D0905113

Founded in 1996
by Toi Derricote
and Cornelius
Eady, Cave Canem
is a workshop/
retreat for African
American poets
and is dedicated
to nurturing and
celebrating African
American culture.
Cave Canem
sponsors a poetry
prize for the best
original manuscript
by an African
American poet
who has not yet
been professionally
published.

WINNER OF THE 2006 CAVE CANEM POETRY PRIZE

a gathering
of matter
a matter
of gathering

a gathering
of matter
a matter
of gathering

POEMS BY DAWN LUNDY MARTIN

The University of
Georgia Press
Athens and London

Publication of this volume has been made possible
in part by The Ford Foundation. Additional thanks
to Lannan Foundation for organizational support.

Published by The University of Georgia Press
Athens, Georgia 30602
www.ugapress.org
© 2007 by Dawn Lundy Martin

Poems originally published in *Callaloo*, "Violent Rooms"
(23.1 [2000], 221), "The Morning Hour" (22.4 [1999],
1016–18), "Bearers of Arms: 1775–1783" (23.1 [2000],
222–23), and "Sunday Lessons" (23.1 [2000], 216–17),
© Charles H. Rowell. Reprinted with permission
of The John Hopkins University Press.

Designed by Mindy Basinger Hill
Set in 10/15 pt Adobe Garamond

Most University of Georgia Press titles are
available from popular e-book vendors.

Printed digitally

Library of Congress Cataloging-in-Publication Data
Martin, Dawn Lundy.
A gathering of matter, a matter of gathering :
poems / by Dawn Lundy Martin.
50 p. ; 22 cm.
"Winner of the 2006 Cave Canem Poetry Prize."
ISBN-13: 978-0-8203-2991-8 (pbk. : alk. paper)
ISBN-10: 0-8203-2991-6 (pbk. : alk. paper)
I. Title.
PS3613.A7779G38 2007
811'.6—dc22   2007007191

British Library Cataloging-in-Publication Data available

for my loving mother
and
for my dearest Stephanie

What stripping down
can close the cave of grief?

CONTENTS

Carl Phillips

From the very start of reading Dawn Lundy Martin's *A Gathering of Matter / A Matter of Gathering,* I found myself simultaneously drawn to how language is here deployed on the page, confounded by it, and slowly, steadily instructed by it. Which is to say, I knew I was in the presence of something quite original—and the immediate effect of the original is one of disorientation on the part of the reader. If the work is strong enough, it will make us want to understand it, and we will keep returning to it until we have learned *how* to understand it.

Part of the project of these poems is to enact the very dilemma with which they are wrestling, namely, how to give expression to human experience given how the means of expression—language—is itself suspect. "The language of ordinary life . . . use[s] convention and label to bind / and organize us," says Erica Hunt, as cited in Martin's "A Bleeding, an Autobiographical Tale." And it would seem to be this anxiety about language's ability to impose restriction that alerts Martin to, as she puts it, "[a] need for unrecognizable speech," and from there to the questions "What are the limits of expression? Where does / language go limp, break apart, or fall into pieces, stammers, glimpses, / or just merely the black marks that make up letters?"

One place where this fracturing and stammering would appear to occur is in the wake of what language has wrought at the level of identity—in terms of gender, sexuality, and race in particular—and in terms of how we come to think of the body and, by extension, moral conduct. Many of the poems here suggest a voice that is struggling (up from violence/violation) toward utterance, by fragment, by stammer, by sometimes evolving into articulateness ("Suh—sssuh—ssuck. Insistence. Lips go lisp."), by sometimes making complete sense even as it resists conventional notions of sense ("Is there a blue fiery ice-ice to say this is joy?"), and by sometimes all but shattering in front of us:

[I a-m speak-ing] [langue] [whois] [clivage] [blown]
[fragrance] [deadth] [catefory] [shape] [oh, seet molass]
[brister-breaking] [dainty swerter] [glamos, glamos] [stritening]

Understanding the body as cargo, exposed, buckling, deciduous, "choked
by lust . . . Greased up / and will-less: a drone," how are we to live inside it,
much less speak of it? asks Martin. A similar question arises when she con-
siders the stubborn, irreversible history of American slavery, whose effects
continue to resonate as she remembers the lives of those "who could not
say—who uttered—who died not pronouncing. / From Benin to this frac-
tured exile." Ultimately, Martin seems to take as her subject the overwhelm-
ing human history of violence, of a hatred of difference and a fear of it, of
the desire to erase those whom we deem erasable. Perhaps most disturbingly,
she explores the ways in which society, largely through language's capacity
for definition—which is also, of course, a form of delimitation—can alien-
ate us from our very selves, or bring us to the point of self-hatred and a
desire for self-erasure.

To speak in the face of such a history, even as we suspect that speech itself
may betray us—for indeed, it does—is finally a heroic gesture, tragically
heroic. "[I wanted silence in the flowers, not to not say, but to not have the
impulse of saying.]" is the line with which Martin closes her book, suggest-
ing a desire close to Keats's in his "Ode to a Nightingale" to be all instinct,
stripped of self-consciousness, of which language is a manifestation. But to
face the reality of being alive in language and to choose to make meaning
from the very language that has also been a means of reducing humans to
something less than human, these are gestures reminiscent more of Beckett,
with whose late prose (I am thinking here of *Company*, *Ill Seen Ill Said*, and
Worstward Ho) Martin's work shares a similar starkness, a similarly haunted
loveliness, which is all the lovelier *for* its hauntedness. In the end, though,
Martin does what it is in fact the responsibility of the poet to do: she exists
within literary traditions, even as she pushes those traditions further, via
her decidedly original, arresting, no-holds-barred vision. This is an exciting
debut from a poet whose voice I hope will continue to keep defying the very
silence it claims to long for.

ACKNOWLEDGMENTS

Poems in this book first appeared, sometimes in different versions, in the following publications: "The Symbolic Nature of Chaos" in *Encyclopedia, vol. 1: A–E* and reprinted in my chaplet, *The Undress* (belladonna #89); "After the Death of a Young Poet," "After Drowning," and "Every Man, Woman, Child" in *nocturnes* 3; "Negrotizing in Five; or, How to Write a Black Poem" is forthcoming in *Breakfast and Blackfist: Notes for Black Poets*, edited by Thomas Sayers Ellis; "Blackface Caricature in Thirteen" in my chapbook, *The Morning Hour* (Poetry Society of America); "Telling Tales" in *nocturnes* 1 and reprinted in *The Morning Hour*; "[. . .]" in *Crossroads* (Fall 2003); "Violent Rooms," "The Morning Hour," "Bearers of Arms: 1775–1783," and "Sunday Lessons" in *Callaloo* and reprinted in *The Morning Hour*; "A Bleeding, an Autobiographical Tale" in *FENCE* and reprinted in *The Morning Hour*; "Unspeaking" in *The Sour Thunder: A Net Opera*, edited by Mendi+Keith Obadike, and reprinted in *The Morning Hour*; "Bone" in *The Morning Hour* and reprinted in *Crossroads*; "The Undress" in *The Undress*.

a gathering
of matter a matter
of gathering

LAST DAYS

What is the relation between Figure A and Figure B?

This is what the father has become.

That which is gone already?

Two feet, white with calluses, miasmic.

Who breathes in the room?

A girl on the bed, a daughter.

Only one then?

They won't deliver him to her, her palms, little petals.

Untouched?

Untouched. Yes.

Will they arrive then?

The wilting body is unmade on a soiled bed.

What color is the cusp of absence?

A selfish collection of coins in the dresser drawer.

Mine come that way.

A redefinition of what smell is.

Is there a terrible thing?

There are A and B and some curtains drawn tight to lock the room.
There is the scent that I will remember for many years.

This is what happens before the figure disappears?

A row of unkempt stones they call heroes.

How is the pain endured?

A stem of grass imagined when it is not raining.
All those things called intentions. The private treasures one keeps safe.

THE SYMBOLIC NATURE OF CHAOS

There were robberies and thieves, deft cutting into and savaging,
portents like a yelling and a tree. What would come now
that the drifting had begun? Now that the swinging, inconsistent
with landscapes [what cyclones left] in the darkness of this bereft body.
A thing ungroomed.

Hears the butcher. Bends into supplication. The meat of the body. Series of punctures, microscopic holes. Pungent. Perpendicular. Constructed as likeness.

Fabrication. It emits. It gags. Streams into lips, slightly, unconsciously parted. Putrid breath escapes, unbeknownst.

Amid this fury, she wrote me a love letter. She said, "If you were here I wouldn't miss you this much." She said, "There is cauliflower growing amongst what has been planted."

The body bends down so the wrists are at the ankles. Exposed. Buckling.

[a matter of gathering

[the stray, unremarkable—

the reason of wings, you'll notice.

Amid some beauty, one wall, for example, paved in patterned red
paper. Of please, please, I'm waiting. To cut. [This is a cutting.] And run.
Skin is felt, is raised, surfaced. Pulling down into haggard drown.
The stench of one's own desire. They call and call from dark channels,
by hoards, knowing this—her viscera.

Her blue mound, a sapling. One remembers the gesture of a deep
footstep, the legs only, extending as if in awe. One remembers
the gutted *r*'s and *o*'s, the white haw, like my devil,
like the devil I keep.

[I said to her "maybe" and "if it comes," "interesting" and "possibility." I said, "I want, I want" and "what if."] [She wanted to know about lying. I said no. She wanted to know about trust. I said trust is relative. She wanted me to love her. I said I did but did only in the way that all things are palatable.]

One is bowed. Cranked. One ciphers.
You can hear it over the trees at night. Things are forgotten.
Become unknown. Absent as in synapsed void. Someone is
debased. A strict figure designed for fucking. Deciduous.

There could be divisions. Latent fallacies, facial twitches, when the *I* spoke, when it said, *I am the yearner.* It set out, through decades, brushed by stray bristles, poked at and prodded. *I am the yearner,* it repeated. Graceless figure, unexuberant claws.

They say there are no dolls. It is night. I wander. The body
wants. Is choked by lust. Occupied fully, mechanically. Greased up
and will-less: a drone.

(Ambling toward tall green
and black desert of trees.
In the wind, leaves clack
too rapidly. Are they hovering?)

They say lust is a sin, *concupiscence of the flesh*. Flesh of
formidable volume. Listens attentively. Near gleeful. Exhumes.
Must smell of it. Where reek inhabits particularity. A glass of red wine
on the breath. Tell me what happens. What happens in a dark park
on the edge of this debilitating desire?

solemnity of fish
there were no dancers
understand this
do not weep
do not weep
from the belly
from the bowels
what is anger?
where does the deep end?
there were walls here
housed like fruit in skin
it ripped
hum of traffic
lull of striptease
what happened three decades ago?
there is an end to this story?
(wrap it up)
say grace and everything
padlock the door
when leaves fall from trees
when birds can be heard a mile away
here, like a dove in hand
(mystery obscured)
so white
so white with filth
what I will say to you will not be heard
it will be unnatural
it will be like something opening up
a row of corpses
proportionless
I want to tell you of my perennial
gracelessness, of an epithet hunger
of a joy that is neither sadness nor joy
a joy that is a rung of teeth
say something

AFTER THE DEATH OF A YOUNG POET

Blood shed and wasted. Blood resonating, a sting. Found them in a puddle of it. Positioned as if they had been planted—had placed themselves—so that the puddle made a pond for them to lie in. So that brown bodies rested preternaturally still in a red pond in a house on a floor. Someone—a great distance away—rang and rang and rang, and then walked away. Someone else—later—thought and then said *wasteful* and *shame*.

NEGROTIZING IN FIVE; OR,
HOW TO WRITE A BLACK POEM

Formlessness.
One enters an unforgiving, inchoate world. No mold to make,
fossilizing. Here is the secret: I cannot tell you because it is not known.
My fingers obtund with effort. One asks about stuff, considers what
comes next, is maddened by possibility. Some castigating black marks
condition the body, soften the skin, open into sepulcher. But the
body will not be buried there. It will put down a thing on a page,
emancipated [nearly] by the imagination.

Mutilation.
Hands are scarred, almost dead. You bleed from the knees, ruddy,
feebly scratch out signs including As if. You are on the floor. You plead.
You make filth. What to bare out? What to pitchfork? You want to
be rid of the black. And you want to embrace the black. You write,
Grandmother, and cross it out. You peel. You acknowledge the pain of
peeling. You are hollowing in, coarse carving a sound to resemble that
which must be said. You drag your canvas over and finally write with
whatever fluid has spilled.

Sing a song that cannot be sung.
A maw. A silence. It wanted to say, I am, but said instead, It was.
Noted the skin's purple hue, fell into longing, thought of what was
made and what was done. Went to speak and said, Sith sith, and then,
Mmmoss. Finger pointed at the body and then at the sun, realized
nothing and fell again taciturn. There was, too, a craving: a stale
remembrance that came a jolting. A hard feeling, a swallowed rock.
Wanted to wrench a cavity and pull, expose the stone, as if I could, but
could not.

I/M/A/G/E.

Tell me—I am telling you—the scent of your coming down, breath already at my belly button, easing. Or the black room of terror that you half-recall, half-invent. Tell me of the exact moment you slashed through your surprisingly tough skin with a pocketknife and how it felt like rain. I want to tell you about the splitting of a female body—how I squeezed into it—fitting barely, of the texture of melancholy, of a sycophantic love, draw a flicker for you, let you enter as if entering me.

Completion cleaved.

All that has been spoken. All that threatens the legitimacy of that which is attempting to be said. Phonemic struggle—I'll call it a precursor to blathering. Scintilla. Something dragged in the sand. An ocean of debris. In the instants before arrivals some things happened. What is perpetually almost, spilling off its imagined page, signaling an infinite number of openings, leakages, stuck tongues. Blath, said by mistake, and begun again. Bath, said clearly. But, in the end, blath returned more persistently [unofficially], because it was dirty.

BLACKFACE CARICATURE IN THIRTEEN

1. Capsule of exile.
2. Her body in sway.
3. Garment of rust and patches.
4. She imagines herself peeling a thick-skinned orange.
5. Dense-scented epiderm.
6. Missive uncovering large flank.
7. Milk.
8. Oh, children, children.
9. Cluck in frontier of, cluck cluck cluck.
10. Ground upon which to gaze.
11. Craning the neck to see back of head.
12. Hummmmm-ing.
13. Come muslin, come drift, deep dirt, grand mass, and crescendo.

AFTER DROWNING

To part pinprick, pry back
kind resistance, develop it, and
say something
incomprehensible.
She put on her soft body. She
was grafted in particulars,
patterns a distinct location, a
place various, more various,
she said, and in saying,
spilled over into the body's
many parts. Fell for the sake
of it, and found there at the
bottom of the pit a stool to
sit on, a hand to ring. [Palate
spun.] A thing pernicious.
Perceived as such and was
such, dangled on the tip of
stick, drip.

She curdles in the kraal. Could lactate, only stopping when the being is full up. Penned in with foal, with fur. Dereliction impossible, yet the thing. The one absolution from the designed body. As if one could locate, here in the barnyard, a logic, a wonder, a stabbing toward datum, corpus. What is it like to feel female? Explicitly? A body that feeds. Is food. Is gnawed on. One that kneels. A facilitator. Organized joy. A corporeal caving in, arranging the joist. Cooing.

She said, when I fuck them, I think I can make them love me.

I said, when I fuck them, I think I can get something back.

What is mumbled after the act? I—Uh. After the craving empties. When viscosity permeates a life before. Magenta. And, falling there, through sound, through tape, a voice ghostly, saying blackly, I bleed. This is what it takes. I hear it now. Know it. There was once a time when the bridge ended and the girl leapt. There was once a singing somewhere.

Once upon the unsung,
the ripped and the extracted,
one would arrive at thinning
trees (the trees are almost
naked), opening of leaves,
and thick scents—
one would be summoned
there and anchored.

Believe that one travels in articulation, is heavy with language, is
hunted, breathes and hears black bitch and black ass in the literal field of
the carnivorous.

What would be sought for and fetched?
One's desire accumulates in pustules.

A precise dictation occurs inside the chest. It is a reckoning with a kind
of god, a kind of believing.

Wizened plastic wire sings a terrible lullaby. The body will ripen.
Will become slippery, slope over into exigent sickness. Reeds will recede.
Caps will lift. And in the heart of it, she will lie down on newly woven
cloth and scrub what has already been scrubbed: a gentle body, smooth
from touch.

Wide eyes, all white and glistening. Gradual induction into a bare, still damp, secreting pact. The body hammering. Hammered.

Awoken to the second door, the closed one. She focuses on the sofa's hem, unlatches the rung of locks, rejecting catapult.

It was a brown room,
wood-paneled,
an attic room,
cut into by the glaring
television, pared like sleeves,
stank as funk stinks,
as the nearly dead,
as the red red red,
as dripping old eyes,
it was a late December sky,
the hallway led to the
bathroom,
the waiting,
a tall glass, my departing.

MIRROR, MIRROR

Before then.

Stigma etched. What the water cannot drench or salvage. Had it been here before this descending form, this wretched girl, spun in a desperate attempt to see her own face?

Once, before this moment, a girl, a girl unknown to anyone, brushed off her knees. The sun was hot. She ignored the sun, her knees imprinted by gravel, leapt toward something that appeared to be the sun, but was not, was something imagined, a thing unclaimed, unsealed, no warning in sight.

BUTTERFLIES BECOME

for Anne Sexton

What steeled?

[Fatwa] [Faucet of defiance] [From mesa]
[Desert stinge] [Vulva stiffening] [Sulfuric blunder]
[Bleat—for suffering] [Breasts growing like corn]

> All the pretty ones will lose their heads,
> will locket the precious,
> will enter the space of the dying
> and the dead.
> Bend over, dear one,
> raw horse, one stag,
> one back buttressed,
> ready like soft wax.

BONE

They say, recovering, lips suffering the glass. And they say,
>   dig, dig, rise from tough root.
To know is to know why, or was. Was meant? Was granted.
>   Was ungrateful. Holes that stick,
that permeate holes. Sufficient consequence. Working the
>   loom. Yards of it. Sprawling, choking.

Toward him. When sleep comes, it comes bare. Barely.
>   To balance there. *It has been twenty years.*
"What do you think about when you think about him?" Only,
>   toward him. Brush of him. Breath brush. Rum.
It was my first drink. Hairless arms and legs. Breath
>   of drink. Breath. Barely breast.

Rehearsal. The economy of fawn. "What do you play when
>   you replay?" Wet slabs of heat. What it is to
be cornered. Teeth against knees. Sufficient unmaking.
>   It's an old joke: don't take candy from
strangers. Stranglers. A category of depthness. Endless
>   layering. First, second, third . . . like that.

The other side of once. Beckoning. Called if. Hating if only.

THE UNDRESS

They say, erased.

Someone once said, once sung, a lament for the destruction of the
beautiful. Emblem brandished upon entrance into tribe. He spoke two
words I did not understand. I think he said it's hateful or it happened.

That the body—trespassed—troped—made haven—made him awful—
deeply recognized. He unraveled—epithelium peeled—pelted first,
then simply removed. He was what we might call—would
most likely call—an ugly, black man.

To dance, he thought, in the cover of night, finally unseen.

He wore robes.

He untied his robes.

Let them fall gracefully to the floor.

Some kind of spiral, he thought,
some kind of mirror for my lakes of grief.

They say, betrayal.

He had undone it, reversed time, made no allowances, poured it all
into a stinking black bowl.

> [What human form sleeves out of]
>
> [An imagining outside itself]
>
> [A grasping of the garrote]
>
> [A phylum called unsatisfactory]

The meat is work.

Porous skin finally gone, gouged. He no longer sings gospel but hums
silently in his head, *What I have done, what I have done.*

[One can hear it falling]

[Pecked out of order]

[Racing in a circumference]

[To be not forgotten]

Upon driving on an absent road, the body shivers. Resonates itself.
Dittos for a moment. Incision cut [niggardly] [whimsical] and let go,
pleads, Let me go. Struggles with wretchedness, attempts to scream,
curls back into, settles [settles as butterfly would].

I am unpractical, wanting desire.

Not to be fragrant. To be raw. A bone.

Not to bend. To slumber.

They say, love your body, love yourself.

Have seen the blur of it. Have endured cosmology. As a crack on a wall
endures flawlessness.

When the basement sweats, a mental note: the body is not
indestructible. Click. One can create erosion. O, my tin cup is too
full—it smothers—I stumble, stammer, the word, *strings*.

Had a body with blood in it. Blood that stinks, comes in tumors, drops as pennies drop.

Had turned monstrosity, from fledging thing, weak, to vague resemblance of human tissues. (To burn, to blast, to shell, to cut.) To blaze, to deep entirety, his leaves gone back black, gangs that leapt gnashing into the surface of what could be human form.

Genus: speculation.

When the wax dries, finally, alongside the glass,
what rises when the dead are buried?

I happened. Someone happened. We might call it a happening—
breathing, living beings gathered—
brought together as if drunk—as if unbroken,
as if able to speak against fraught with—washed over.

Somewhere, a dog stands alone on a street at night.

In the war, a woman soldier is taken hostage and no one
will say what happened.

There are empty hands pissing. A matter of folding clothes,
of waiting.

When we are lost and mute. When we are sold into strangeness.

[Hole dug in] [Strong desire to speak] [Categories of silence]
[Asphyxiation] [Bloating from here] [Asphalt] [Mouth full of bees] [The
body castrate] [A bright, white day] [If only a signal, a breaking—does it
splinter? In reverence?

In increments, a seeping—that multiple hands will
attempt to cover.]

There are mothers who are already buried.

There are mothers who never sung.

[. . .] *

I am trying to write a story of my father's impending death. Its largeness.
I step into the breach (or is it a presence?), pull it, seeping, through the
skin. It opens—the body—fractures, becomes less a body. *He is small.*
An unnatural child. The skin sags off the bones; the bones retreat. It is in the
eyes, I think. *They are soft. They are for the first time gentle*—the hardness of
silence, its tremendous matter, the nothing that is some thing, and of its
coming.

I capture a witness / a reader in order to say, in order to be able to say,
that I cannot say. See. *In an old photograph, my father is a man. Broad*
shouldered. He poses behind the bar, smiling. A cigarette casual between the
fingers. The image is seamless, finished, a white border encloses it. I think,
he has never told me about the war. I am trying to write the story of my
father's life. Hot iron poking the same black spot. Quantities of sore. See?
Dogs circle a whining prey. Indescribable prey.

VIOLENT ROOMS

1.

The contours of the girl blur. She is both becoming and fact.
A rancor defines the split. Rip into. Flatten the depth of voice. That

urgent flex peels off the steady layers. A girl, I say.
Girl. Gu-erl. Quell. He. He—unbuttons before emergence.

As in yard rake pressed to roof of mouth. A fragrant rod.
Suh—sssuh—ssuck. Insistence. Lips go lisp. Our brutish boy.

Having not ever been whole. Or simple. Or young. Just split and open.
Not of it. For it. Born a cog of hard wheel at five, six, seven . . .

What to know of what has never been?

2.

No common place would do: bar stool, front porch, sea rock.
Such a room should crawl into the soul. Stretch it. Contort it.

Could be the straddle of this stranger at the neck. *I am this.*
She does not waver. She is twenty-five. The bed is wet. As many

as had done this thing before. The wound is rupture. Blood-faced.
Between sailing and anchor. No, between shipwreck and burial.

What does the mouth do? It does not mean no, saying no.
It does not mean yes. It gurgles. It swells. It is comfort.

A quick kick. Mighty, mighty.   29

THE MORNING HOUR

And these hands my mother's

        Washed.

When washing was—when clean could not be.
To wrap the body in cotton.   What imprisons.

        When carrying humped—

and these bald knuckles from her.
The lips tight. Damp.   This Desire.

Beyond that.   A tiny voice.

The foreign woman
who bends over—is spotted.
Her wind is taken.

              [   ]

A closed back.   Turned in.   Centered.   A world shut out.
The infinite lines welt.   Her voice is open.   Transparent.
Dissolved.   A tunnel protector.   A subtle skin.   *Olivia.*

Hold these shoes to the sun. They are just shoes.
What the girl has not. How secret the burden. Carrying nothing.
And common.   Breathe.

This moment open.   She wrenches.   Falls into—
this small casing inflamed.   She scrubs.   And is common.

[   ]

What did Negro *replace?*
    Claiming what could have been.
    Their strange feet making a way.

And what metaphor?
What could call the horrors?

Pressing hands we cannot decipher.
An arched woman hunches in.
Presence.   Birth.   Our bracelet.

Who navigated wooden ships?
    This hardened ankle sucks black earth.
    Her slight life.

Help us poison position.
And Olivia, the mouth of his children
from the mouth of my vagina.
And Olivia, what no memory can recall
lost eternally inside covered wagons.

       [   ]

Walk eternities. Feet thick as throats.
What will become a life.

When do voices gain earth?
The finest grain solved between the thumb and forefinger.
Reads like the slightest movement of a hip.

And nothing is left but time. And God. And the dense night.
Against skins.

What is simple
is nothing.

Imagine history.
An entire race
looks into
the slit camera eye.

[   ]

Speak of going back,
of gathering the horses,
the prized memoirs
that have nothing to do with place.
and pack like a boy
who leaves his slivered home.

About land.

What is familiar
is the warm spice
of a girl oiled
in lavender.

Into oceans.

Lie and almost remember—
almost breathe soiled air and ire.

Count foreign.
Make sense
of the sounded boots
that exhaled fate.

[   ]

The footsteps are wet. Desire is wet.
Is going step by step—
the ash trail is wicked. The thicket wept.

Must be quieted—that vast space between the—there.
These tittied deities—Our Orishas—
how they seized what they did not know.

Every element is bare. Like ruptured mouths—
who could not say—who uttered—who died not pronouncing.
From Benin to this fractured exile.

                    I am in this fist.
                    I am a witness in exile.

Our old. Two settlers. Claiming Land. The collective hum.
A distant Lord Missy. And this huge hand reaches beneath the skin.
Want is _____. I am hot inside the bone.

Believe this exit.   Take. Take. Take.

UNSPEAKING

Zero as the translation of O. The circle a mouth makes in pronouncing.
O. *I have never told anyone this before.* It is ruby. Rubbed. Spot that throbs
and gapes. Sound of the O. On my skin (it has a surface) I inscribe with a
hot clip the letters of a puncture. *Deserted carousel. Headless horse.*

The fit is tight. Splitting into—stiff cup. A dark mouth moves, enters
the tremor of a voiced Uh. But, all this is not love, not love in the way
one milks the center. Instead, chronic terror stripped to bone grating
upon bone. Of down home, twang twang, and promise. *My knees pressed
behind ears.*

Between poundings, the body Uhs. Cracked R. Cracker, crack her.
Laughing: you ain't nothing but a black maid. The process is a patient
body, waiting for discovery, hovering, crissed, saying, *Christ.*
This is raw data. Standing broken, the udders flap. He grunts: *Is this
what you want, whore?*

Swimmingly. Neck drooped. One attempt. Another. *This is a very private
moment.* Zero as the incarceration of a theme. Uh, and Uh again. Peels
the pink inside of the cheek. As if hollowing out. Hollering a big giant O.
There is the saw sawing and the needle pinning. *I wait. Unspeaking.*

[Signal] [A black thought] [Black as in a tunnel darkening] [A secret]
[Cranked] [Red] [Sense of unmoving] [Pleasure of seeing a dead thing]
[Female as in floating, floating] [Whispering] [Muh]

EVERY MAN, WOMAN, CHILD

1.

Where they were stuck,
as if by quickened breath.
A riddle of them
lined on a fence.
Manes of hair.
Lost lips loll in the grip
of those who would take aim.

Where they were felled.
Where salt had been made.
Columns. Land of verdict.

Where ballads would be sung.
Reverberation in the hole of unlit night.
Language of machete.
Bodies like stalks (reeds).

> *I was a farmer and lived.*
> *There were leeches in the march.*
> *It was impossible.*
> *They were investigating.*

An arm rises out of the mud (as if growing there).

There were and then there were not.
[Puzzle and topple] [Lift and intersect]

2.

Over a precipice, into the dark.

Effort in finishing them.

He would return to the place he had never been.
A place where five niggers or gooks or spics huddled
under the wettest sky you ever saw. Return and say,

Here I am not accused. Here I am not.

Fins of fish. Floral of fish. Fishing for information.

No one remembers the effort in the killing,
that the body has resistances, and caves in
only when significantly battered.

Who would listen to the story of one who was not there,
one who returned to the place of naught, one black river,
one blood gut, one final mystery, a turning that tunneled
(trenchant) (tremored) and ending up against—

Some old fingers touched him. (He did not want to be touched.)

INSTRUCTIONS

Sunday. A tea towel folded into halves, then quarters, to make her a
pillow. The head barely hung—it happened gently, tactile fusion of wit
and tenderness—mine—an artifice woolen—*I only wanted to break,
like splinters would be evidence.* It was not a gift. The project. Languish.
Fullness. Imagine her surrounded by toads and a pen.

FIRE ISLAND

Summer 2005

It lies down as it has always lain down,
floating into the blank light of the deep sea.

She unremembered here. A pounding, sucking force—
think about the water's white rim.

When open, not as cavern, as rice.

Back first, arms lax and extending, hair ascends as dust,
only an outline of what once was, blurred deeply, plunging
colorless against expanse, devoid of scent, devoid of air. She is full.
She has been filled in vines and photographs.

BEARERS OF ARMS

1775–1783

Body-cargo.

Organs rise to forefront of skeletal cave.

From dust to this

damp, wooden cavity.

        What worth in bones and flesh?

Cartographers ready. It will begin here and end there.
Continents new with boot prints.

Land cleared of human-refuse. That one can make another into.
And become root-torn, clown-face, muled-man.

◎◎◎

The body grows out of an ear.   *Savage.*

Too conspicuous in tall grass.   *Native.*

Incongruent sounds erupt from mouths.   *Speaks a vulgar tongue.*

Stored in Jefferson's house—like so many paper boxes in pantry.

That skin which absorbs sunlight

could stand to deaden, be deadened.

Looming sickle, patient.
        Run.
Something deliberate at risk.
        Run.
Hint given.
A song no longer a song.

To where cities were not yet built.

In honor of dirt roads that will become.

What idea in that hope of institutions?

The bitter irony on tongues
rips at what would be comedy
to join the chant
"liberty, liberty"
in "thoughtless imitation."

Men with hands that look like men's hands.

Skins silken in southern sun. Not an absence of. Excess.

This equation:
Two hundred freed, four thousand enslaved.
Hands that can wave, but do not.
Feet that are not silent, but dare not speak.
Quest of interior articulated in dead darkness,
candelabra burning in farthest corner.   40

This reprisal.
Lone pen scratches fortunes onto meaningful paper.
         Deal scratched in whole of throat.
         An exchange for being executioner.
Had worn uniform with flag,
bore down into grunting earth,

         for tentative freedom.

A BLEEDING, AN AUTOBIOGRAPHICAL TALE

1.

On the knees sucking a pestle. [Gripped in particular horrors:
the stinked history of other inappropriate drills—being a girl.] Becomes
revolving locale, cataclysmic obsession, a time-warp nightmare. In
motel rooms: a ditty, a slim filth; asking questions such as when does
one become whole, gentle whore? [Unfillable state.]

2.

Which language rankles? Unsettling the tub of tummy? Sssith. Frozed.
Sentenced. Fabric that is not fabric. A need for unrecognizable speech.
Resisting the tyranny of the prosaic, the beautiful, the poetic utopia.
"The language of ordinary life . . . use[s] convention and label to bind
and organize us."[1] What are the limits of expression? Where does
language go limp, break apart, or fall into pieces, stammers, glimpses,
or just merely the black marks that make up letters?

3.

A crooked finger pointing. Over there. No. There. No there.
Approximation. Blurred vision. Attempt after attempt into oblivion.
Opening and opening. This body is a cave. "To attempt becomes
liberation."[2] The metaphor is a long process, an indefinite gesture,
undone by any bell-ringing clarity. That's crystal clear. It's crystal.

4.

Is there a blue fiery ice-ice to say this is joy?

5.

I am speaking. I assert this. I must assert this. Entering into all that has already been said, written, carved into stone, reproduced, and reiterated into the very cellular makeup of the body. Ontology? [Strict, but not forgiving.]:

Could not tell   in the swarm   what sound would be.

Bearing responsibility. A rock. To pull up from the layers of muck and shit some utterance, some something that does not stitch me pinup doll, black rabid, black snatch.

6.

Emergence on the outside. Fly. Spot. Chimera. Writing into—

7.

Dancing here, too. Paly. Play. Which came first the black or the nigger? Who is reflected in "nigger jim" of the fat black smiling "mammy"? What is seen? The self. Or hate. Rippled soldiers "that can be made, out of a formless clay, an inapt body."³ [*Performing gentle strokes to measure and erase the brute. Earthy, not licentious. A goodness. A black pride. Attempt at exorcism.*] A niggarealness. Impossibility of erasure. To purge, instead, by erupting, comforting, lifting to surface.

8.

[I a-m speak-ing] [langue] [whois] [clivage] [blown]
[fragrance] [deadth] [catefory] [shape] [oh, seet molass]
[brister-breaking] [dainty swerter] [glamos, glamos] [stritening]

9.

When a father beats his own son. "(Hint: breath from wood,
swinging.)"[4] The boy on the floor: "(Envisage: cock and dung heap.)"[5]

10.

OOOOOOOOOOOOOOOOOOOOOOOOOOOOOOOOOOOOOOOO
OOOOOOOOOOOOOOOOOOOOOOOOOOOOOOOOOOOOOOOO
OOOOOOOOOOOOOOOOOOOOOOOOOOOOOOOOOOOOOOOO
OOOOOOOOOOOOOOOOOOOOOOOO

Notes

1. From Erica Hunt's essay "Notes from an Oppositional Poetics," published
   in *The Politics of Poetic Form: Poetry and Public Policy*, ed. Charles Bernstein
   (New York: Roof Books, 1990).
2. From a 1999 interview with Myung Mi Kim conducted by Dawn Lundy
   Martin, unpublished.
3. From Michel Foucault's *Discipline and Punish* (New York: Vintage, 1995),
   originally published in France in 1975.
4. From "(Narrative Frame) for My Brother's Story," by Dawn Lundy Martin,
   unpublished.
5. Ibid.

SUNDAY LESSONS

Larger than what they hold.
     Bulbous.
Too gentle.
     They reach inside the mouth.
Guarded   locked   hidden
     beneath tongue.

     As if cure.

     Undoing.
Hands pull against seam.
     Part what resists.
Maze of thread-weave.
     The tender rim.
Beneath skin, bones, teeth.

     Unfinished.
When girl was lifted as skirts are.
     Soiled and torn, ankles black,
bare, skinny.
     Preference still.
Voice empty.
     Saying   this happened
and this   and this.

How many bodies is it
     from the basement
to the church
     to singing hallelujah?

The mother's hand
     holds the wrong tool,
undoes the cape,
     tightens the tarp,
encloses fist,
     wedges grip.

Scars are ellipses on face.

To puncture and to welt it.

Could tell those travels.

Direct at blood-beat angled as to cease it.

Wanting a single occasion,
     leg cramp
     found wallet
     stillbirth

or just to be a boy.

Walks up the narrow staircase
     to top of lighthouse,
waves crash the air tight

in fist   after fist.
Longing for all that depth,
      that eternal distance.

Erupts from the belly like the letter *G*.
      Teeth come together in grit.
The bottom row pressed neat behind
      the upper mount.
Tongue flexing as if in fucking
      or the razor intentional on flesh.

The body is so small.

How could—

I was a girl once as free as a boy.
As certain as hot light in summer.
Desiring Daedalus's craft.

A MYTHOLOGY OF MELANCHOLY

They were afraid.
Rightly, they thought,
rough heads bobbing in agreement.

One drew a skeleton on his chest.
Another thought of mythic forests.

His to imagine, original.
Deftly as sense—a coming season—
he drew down into the crypt of
what had been, spoke into the middle ear,
said, "Ruck," said, "Crutch," said, "Wandering."

There were sounds not in the body. Sounds in the distance.
Made the body understand what it is to hear,
to know something outside itself.

It stood naked in the frequency. It drank in relation.

TELLING TALES

Egg shells	crisp
a fetish	(in wind)
wide	across ridge roof mouth.
Subtle	on wire skin.

My skin.	In darkness.	Knows fingers.
Scratched.		
Not of the body.	Bodied (bloodied).	Blanketed.
Weight.	Shroud me.	*Shush.*

An angry metal on tongue—
tenuous sentences trail in air.
A girl crawls along a wall's edge.

It's seasonal, play.	Played with.
	Teased.
	Teaser.

Not the hands this time.

| No palm open | bent backwards |
| into naked | as if lying. |

Like veins tell stories.

| The trace of them. | The glare of them. |

Their inflamed swagger.

Almost utters *here's the tongue's belonging.*

What there is reached for.

Cut

                sift

                ringed.

And let slip   peeled texture

    sift—

that makes in hot.   And sidewalk summers

like hopscotch   lips/him/stick/break   break   break.
That jump rope—   weapon/undo/loose/lose

and wait   until the sun goes down

and pinch the tight wads of carpet between your legs.

Could wash. Could go over you. Could be like soldier boys

that not knowing which sword. And swamp fever. That go.

I get undressed in strong light. My skin like the wrong clothes.

I am without flesh in the heat of.

Some blue feet
in fallen leaves.